S0-AJZ-611

NOAH'S ARK

Georgie Adams

Illustrated by Anna C. Leplar

BROADMAN
&HOLMAN
PUBLISHERS

The story of Noah and his amazing ark
is from the Old Testament, in the Bible.

Long ago, when the world was quite new, a man named Noah lived with his wife, their three sons, Shem, Ham, and Japheth and their wives. Noah and his family worked hard and tried to live the way God wanted them to.

But God looked around the world and saw everyone else behaving badly. People were fighting, quarreling, and killing each other, or they were stealing from their neighbors, or being cruel to their animals. Not surprisingly, it made God sad.

God decided he must do something.

"Because things have gone very wrong in the world," he said
to Noah. "I'm going to send the biggest flood EVER.
But I will keep you and your family safe.
When the flood is over, I'll start again
with you, and your children."

Noah was just wondering how he would escape from the flood, when God told him. "You must build an ark," he said, "big enough for you and your family. I want you to take on board a male and a female of every kind of bird, animal, and crawling insect. Be sure to take enough food and water too."

Noah listened carefully as God told him the exact measurements, and the kind of wood to use to build the enormous boat. The ark was to have three decks, rooms, a window, a door, and a roof, and it had to be painted with tar to make it watertight.

Phew! thought Noah. What a job!

There was no time to lose. Noah and his family worked from morning 'til night building the ark. Shem, Ham, and Japheth cut down trees, and sawed them into planks. Before long, the boat began to take shape.

While Noah's sons worked on the ark, Noah and his wife traveled far, searching for animals. Mrs. Noah made a list:

cows, sheep, goats, pigs, camels, rabbits, lions, bears, mice, donkeys, elephants, tigers . . .

"Don't forget reptiles, birds, and insects!" said Noah. And he made a list too:

crocodiles, snakes, lizards; parrots, pelicans, ostriches; beetles, bees, ladybirds . . . ants!

Of course, they discovered lots more creatures too. Remember, God had told Noah to find a male and a female of *every* kind. You have never heard so much mooing, roaring, bleating, quacking, squeaking, and cheeping in your life as when Noah brought those animals back to the ark.

There were lots more lists to be made of things they would need for this strange voyage. Things like:

olive oil (for cooking and lamps);

blankets, bowls, and water jars;

barley for making bread;

hay, wheat, and oats;

lentils, leeks, onions, and garlic;

apples, melons, figs, and nuts;

grapes, dates, and pomegranates;

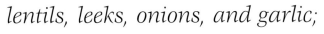

rice, cheese, fish, and meat.

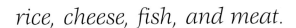

They hoped they hadn't forgotten anything.

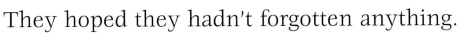

At last the ark was finished. It was gigantic, and smelled strongly of freshly-painted tar. God spoke to Noah and told him that the flood would start in a week. It would rain for forty days and forty nights.

"Time to load up!" said Noah. "It will take a week to get this lot on board."

He was right. It was quite a business getting the animals settled.

As the last two animals trotted up the ramp, Noah felt the first few raindrops on his head. *Plip, plip, plop!* So he took his family into the ark, and God shut the door. The flood had begun.

Imagine what it must have been like. The rain poured down. Rivers overflowed. In the cities, floodwater gushed along the streets. Some people huddled on the rooftops to escape. But the water rose over the houses. Olive trees were uprooted. Fields became lakes, crops were ruined, and sheep, goats, and pigs got swept away in the swirling tide.

Inside the ark Noah heard the rain hammering on the roof. He listened to the water *slap-slap-slapping* against the hull. The ark rose higher and higher—floating over the trees and hills.
As the wind blew and the rain poured, the waves got bigger.

Soon they were drifting over mountain tops. Before long every living thing that wasn't in Noah's ark was drowned.

It rained non-stop for forty days and forty nights, just as God had said.

One morning, about six weeks later, Noah looked out of the window. To his surprise the sun was shining. It had STOPPED RAINING! But still, there was water for as far as his eyes could see.

God sent a strong wind to help blow the waters away. Even so, it took a long time.

Meanwhile the ark drifted about until . . . *bump!* It ran aground on a rock.

Noah looked over the side. "No damage," he said. "But I think we're stuck on a mountain."

And stuck they stayed for many weeks, with water all around. In time Noah sent out a raven, to see if the bird could find dry land. But it didn't.

Noah tried again. This time he sent a dove. The dove flew far and wide, and returned to the ark the same evening. She had found nothing. Noah sent the dove off for the second time, and she returned with a fresh olive leaf in her beak. Somewhere trees were beginning to grow again.

A week later Noah sent the dove out for the third time. He waited all day but she didn't come back. So Noah knew she had found enough dry land to live on.

The next morning Noah looked down the mountain.

"Look!" he cried, "The flood has gone and the land is dry."

The animals were impatient to go outside after all that time in the stuffy old ark. Mrs. Noah lined them up two by two, and led them safely down the ramp. Noah smiled as he watched them go—every pair would make new homes, and begin families of their own.

Then God promised that he would never again send another flood to destroy the world.

"I will give people a sign," said God. "Whenever it rains and there are stormy clouds, I will make a rainbow in the sky. When a rainbow appears, they will know I have kept my promise."

God keeps his promises. There has never been a flood like the one that happened in the story of Noah and his amazing ark.